PASSION!

8 Steps to Reignite Yours

By Mark J. Lindquist

With Jared L. Bye and Patrick O'Shaughnessy

2

PASSION! 8 Steps to Reignite Yours

Step 1: Try a Bunch of Stuff

Step 2: Find Out What You Like

Step 3: Find Your Strength Zone

Step 4: Ask Yourself If You're Passionate About It

Step 5: Don't Stop Until You Find Your Passion

Step 6: Lean-in to Your Passion

Step 7: Take the Money and Run

Step 8: Everything is Possible

Dedicated to:

Aftin, Ainsley and Declan Bye

Pat Bye

Karen O'Shaughnessy

Timothy O'Shaughnessy

Gordon and Diane Lindquist

8

Introduction

I travel all over the nation delivering keynote addresses at corporate conferences and retreats. Almost every other day I am delivering a speech to employees about reigniting the passion that brought them into the workforce in the first place. Without fail, an audience member approaches me after the speech and tells me a story about how they have lost their spark and the twinkle in their eye when it comes to their job.

As I have these conversations with working professionals around the country, sometimes I see a tear welling up in the corner of their eye. They come to me with a measure of despair, as if they have been battling with this issue for quite some time and the speech they just heard has once again exposed the nerve. I would like to think that I understand why they are so emotional about this subject; after all, what we are talking about is a huge part of their lives. The average full-time employee will spend 2,080 hours or more at his or her job each year.

A person's job is the activity that every other activity in their life revolves around. If that person wakes up every morning and doesn't love what they do - that is a difficult reality to face. We talk about their options; we talk about their future. We talk about the sometimes difficult road ahead and the tough choices they will have to make in order to find their passion once again.

CEOs and conference organizers call me up and tell me that their people need a jolt in the arm. The number one issue I'm asked to address as a keynote speaker is to help their people remember why they do what they do. There seems to be an epidemic in the workforce that companies large and small are all facing – their people lack passion.

As a 34-year-old motivational speaker, I have been described as the "Forrest Gump of speakers." They say, "You name it, and Mark has done it." Throughout my journey in 26 countries and all 50 states, I have found a formula for discovering and reigniting your passions in life. It is my hope that this book will assist you on your journey to reignite your own passions at home and at work.

This is a journey I call, "Passion! 8 Steps to Reignite Yours." I hope it helps you become the passionate person we all know you can be.

Your Friend,
Mark J. Lindquist

"Don't believe that the system of success that was handed to you is the best system simply because it was handed to you. What if there was a better way?"

- Mark J. Lindquist

Step 1: Try a Bunch of Stuff

If you want to reignite the passion that brought you into the workforce, then one of the things you'll have to do is push yourself outside of your comfort zone. You're going to have to try. Try is the key word here. If we were all to get honest with ourselves, how often do we try something new? Maybe on our 40th birthdays we decide to try something new. Maybe on New Year's Eve we decide to try something new in the coming year. But as a whole, I'd say that trying new things is just something most of us aren't focused on. We are creatures of habit. Our lives revolve around routines. If you were to line up 100 people in your life from one side of the room to the other, how many people could look you in the eye and say they don't go a day without trying something new? None. Not you, not me, nobody. Once we become adults and build our schedules focused on jobs, kids, activities, etc. our lives just aren't built with room for new things.

After a few years, or maybe it takes 20+ years or more… business professionals find themselves in a room with me. They sit down at a conference or retreat and this kid named Mark J. Lindquist is introduced as their keynote speaker. Many people start off a keynote speech as an audience member with a bit of themselves closed off. I see you, sitting there with your arms folded across your chest, leaned back in your chair with this look in your eye that says loud and clear, "what are you going to tell me that I don't already know?" But I'm a pro. I can take it. My art form is dedicated to breaking through this frigid reception. We spend the first few moments of our time together loosening up those folded arms. We laugh a bit. We warm up to one another. All of a sudden that audience member has changed his outward appearance and now he's leaning slightly forward and nudging his co-worker next to him and they are sharing a laugh. I work extremely hard in the first 20 minutes we have together because I know just how important this hour is. I know that at the end of our 60 minutes those same closed-off audience members will come up to me and talk to me about changing their life.

The process of reigniting your passion begins with a willingness to try. Try what? Try a bunch of stuff. I don't know what career field or industry you're in, but I do know that if you're working to get to the next level, you have to try. You have to embrace a different way of thinking. You have to welcome change. You have to actively seek creativity, ingenuity and imagination. The process of achieving greatness will not necessarily be comfortable nor will it be convenient. However, Step 1 in this process is to try.

You can't tell me that trying is outside the realm of possibility or your capability. We can all try. All it takes is some open-mindedness and some guts. Just try.

I think there's wisdom in this little word: Try.

Take this, for example: You're sitting at the dinner table and you say, "Junior, eat your green beans!"

Junior says, "I don't like green beans!"

You say, "How do you know you don't like them! You haven't even *tried* them!"

How do you know you don't like it, you haven't even tried it?

I believe the beginning of this process to reignite your passion in life is dependent upon your willingness to try. When I'm in front of an audience and we're starting this conversation about passion, I often ask the group to sit down in a quiet moment and write their bucket list. It's a safe moment, they feel comfortable and they are willing to play along with me for a few minutes.

I ask the audience to write down the list of things that they have to do before they kick the bucket. I'm always surprised at how many people have never actually taken the time to write these things down. (Usually, when polled, about 10% of the audience says they have one written down.) Often, I ask the group to write two bucket lists: One that is based on personal desires, and the other that is based on their careers and their companies. I think we all know what a personal bucket list is... but often people haven't been given the chance to write a work bucket list.

I introduce the idea of a work bucket list by talking about the fact that one day you're going to retire from this company. One day you will no longer walk the halls of your organization. What legacy will you leave behind? How will you affect your employee culture? What new level will you lead your people to? How will you position your company within your industry and separate your organization from your competitors? If people have never taken the time to write down a personal life bucket list, even fewer have been given the opportunity to write a work bucket list.

C-Suite leaders come up to me after my speeches or call me months later and they tell me that they were given the opportunity to think differently about their role in the company; that the simple exercise of being in their own personal bubble at a conference room table with no colleagues judging them or influencing their thought process was the difference maker in the next breakthrough idea for their organization.

Think about your average year. How often do you really sit down and take even a few minutes to get yourself in a "bucket list" mindset? In our daily lives we are often too busy to really think long term about our true and deepest desires for our life. At work, our time is consumed by driving schedules, deadlines, to-do's and quarterly goals. Rarely do we have the time to escape, breathe and look at the bigger picture as I ask my audiences to do.

One other important lesson is that I'm not only asking the top level leaders to participate in this exercise – we're also giving that opportunity to the front line employee who has been on the job for three weeks and now gets the chance to come to the annual company conference. New ideas are uncovered in each and every corner of the company and later on in the speech I encourage company leaders to create a culture where there are forums and opportunities to share and communicate these ideas company wide. What if the next multimillion dollar idea just walked in the room in the form of a 23-year-old college grad who just started working for your organization?

Reigniting Passion in Your Personal Life:

Put your 9-5 job aside for a minute. What are the things that you have to try in your life? Did you take a moment to write your bucket list items? You know as well as I do that there is power in writing things down. There are plenty of studies that cite the value of writing your goals: it engages your brain in a different way, it helps you remember, it makes the goal clearer. Play your favorite song and take three minutes to write it down. Open an email, think about what you want to do, experience, or accomplish in your personal life. Jot it down in your phone. Play along with me. What do you have to lose? I always tell my audiences that halfway through this little exercise your brain will try to take over. You'll start thinking this is silly. You'll feel a bit foolish. The logical part of your brain will start to limit your list. Don't allow that to happen. Do whatever you must in order to get in that frame of mind where everything is possible. You have three wishes. You have a magic wand. You just won the lottery. We're talking about expanding the horizons of your future… why not let go of your limiting beliefs and allow your mind to wander into the realm of possibility for a moment?

Reigniting Passion in Your Work Life:

Many of the people I speak to are honest with me as we speak after my keynotes. They have lost the passion for what they do. At work they are going through the motions. It makes me so sad to hear these stories about people who feel stuck. I think you've got two options. Option one: Do nothing. Keep waking up on Monday morning, dreading going into the office. Come home drained with nothing to give to your family and loved ones because it took all your energy just making it to 5:00pm at work. Or you have option two: Try. Try something. Get together with your leadership and have an honest conversation. There's something that brought you into this field and I believe that if you decide you're going to reignite that passion, then there's nothing that can stop you but yourself. There is the person who wakes up defeated and spends the day just waiting for something to happen. Then there is the person who wakes up and decides that they are going to make something happen. What are you going to do to make something happen? Try. Please don't stop trying. Your co-workers need you. Your boss needs you. Even though we're talking about work, your family needs you. The person you married wants to come home to a person who is excited about the next level in his or her career.

Your children deserve to look up at you and see a mother or father who is achieving, striving, growing and learning.

It's time to reignite your passion. I believe that once you have passion for your work, then it overflows to other areas of your life. Right or wrong, in our society what one does for work is such a defining factor of each of us as people. For me, until I had my passion for my career identified, I couldn't truly give my best to the world in the other areas of my life. I encourage you to do the heavy lifting necessary in order to find that passion in your work life. Put yourself outside of your comfort zone; get used to living outside your comfort zone. You'll thank yourself for it.

"Twenty years from now you will be more disappointed by the things that you didn't do than by the ones you did do. So throw off the bowlines. Sail away from the safe harbor. Catch the trade winds in your sails.
Explore. Dream. Discover."

- Mark Twain

Step 2: Find Out What You Like

The first step is try a bunch of stuff. Of that stuff you try, you'll like some of that stuff. Although it seems quite elementary so far, what I'm trying to encourage you to do is expand your horizons, increase your odds of success. If you want to put your scientific hat on for a moment, I'm trying to encourage you to collect enough data about your life in order to call it a legitimate sample. If you were to analyze your life back to your teens or twenties, you probably haven't tried enough things to call it a legitimate sample. If I try one thing and you try 100 things, who is more likely to find the things that they like? Try a bunch of stuff, and of the stuff you try, you'll like some of that stuff. This is the process.

One of the most interesting things I have learned during my time on the road as a motivational speaker comes from Step 2. During this part of my keynote, I ask the audience to write a list of 10 things they like. I don't give any direction or ideas, other than to ask people to list 10 things they like. I play a song and let the audience do the work.

After about 90 seconds I look around the room and it is so interesting to observe the crowd. Pens are stuck in the air at about number 7. At this point, I tell the group, "You may have to dig deep, you may have to think of some things that you haven't done for years. You may have to reach back into your past and dust some things off the shelf to really get to the things that you like."

Once the song is over, I ask the audience to be honest with me. I ask them to raise their hand if they had a hard time getting to 10.

Half the audience sheepishly raise their hands halfway in the air. They look around and breathe a sigh of relief as they realize that many others in the room had the same problem they did completing this simple task. It doesn't matter what room I'm in, whether it be an auditorium of middle school students at a school assembly, a fellowship hall full of little old church ladies, or a room full or business professionals or CEO's from corporate America – they all have a hard time getting to 10. Each and every time it is a third, half, or even two-thirds of the audience that says they had a hard time listing 10 things they like. Amazing. Intelligent grown men and women can't list 10 things they like. In reality, the numbers are probably higher since some people don't participate in the exercise, and some people don't have the guts to raise their hands.

It is the single most interesting discovery of my time on the road as a keynote speaker. It doesn't matter what part of the country

I'm in, or what age or experience level the audience brings to the conversation. We can't list 10 simple things that we like. I think that is a very interesting commentary about how well we know ourselves… or don't know ourselves.

If you can't make a simple list of things you like, then it's no wonder that most Americans aren't doing the things they love. It's no wonder that most of us need to work on reigniting the passion in our lives.

Give it a shot. Play along with me and list 10 things you like.

Keep a list of these things you like:

1. _____

2. _____

3. _____

4. _____

5. _____

6. _____

7. _____

8. _____

9. _____

10. _____

In my life, I have used this list of 10 in good times and in bad. Have you ever felt a little down, a little blue, a little off? Have you ever felt like you were a little depressed or feeling not like yourself? I'm not a clinical psychologist nor am I licensed to give any advice or counsel on such a topic. However, I have found in my life that I can use this list of 10 things I like in order to bring myself out of the dumps.

Think about the last time you were feeling a little blue. I'll bet that if you were to take your list of 10, it probably has been quite a while since you touched that list. It's one of the simplest strategies for a happier life that I have ever implemented in my own life. Feeling blue? Start at number one on your list and I'll bet that by the time you get down to number 5 or 6 on the list, you'll feel a little better. Why? You're doing the things you like. When you're doing the things you like, you smile, you feel better, you are having fun. Give it a shot. This simple strategy has helped me on my journey and I hope it helps you.

If you don't know what you like, then start back at Step 1 and try a bunch of stuff. Of the stuff you try, you'll like some of the stuff. Now you're one step closer to finding the things that you are passionate about, and the things that you love. Want to reignite your passion? Start with finding the things that you like.

"The two most important days in your life are the day you are born and the day you find out why."

- Mark Twain

Step 3: Find Your Strength Zone

I'll bet that some of the things on your list of 10 are there because you are good at them. Some of the things on your list of 10 are an early indicator of the things that you might be passionate about.

Bestselling leadership author John Maxwell explains the strength zone concept like this. Everyone is on a scale of 1-10 with the things that they do. By the time you reach maturity, the most you'll rise on the scale is probably one or two points. Here's an example. If you're a 4 in volleyball, if you put all your time and energy and effort into volleyball, then you may rise to a 5 or a 6. On the flip side, if you're an 8 in football, if you put all your time and energy and effort into football, then you may rise to a 9 or a 10. Maxwell says, "People won't cross the street for 5's and 6's. But they'll cross oceans and stand in line around the block for 9's and 10's."

Business leaders, listen up. What are you doing to ensure that your people are engaged in their strength zone? During my keynotes I see the light bulbs turn on at this point in the speech. Managers and leaders lean back in their chair and they start staring at the ceiling for a moment as if they're drifting into a world of thought and analysis about their own companies and teams. I ask if their company culture is set up in a way that allows employee progression beyond their current position and toward their true strength zones. What does the employee's five-year plan look like? Are we allowing our people the opportunity to try new things, expand their horizons, work through the process of finding out what they like and what they're good at? What we want is a workforce full of people who are giving us their very best they have to give. We want an entire company of people who are giving us their 9 and 10. When I ask the question to the audience at a corporate conference or annual meeting, there are many moments where business leaders look hard in the mirror and realize that there are a few changes that need to be made. More often than not, I find that my friends and peers enter into a company and are expected to thrive in the original department they entered on their first day of work, without being given the chance to find out if that was the best they had to give.

I'm not the best motivational speaker, singer, entertainer, or National Anthem singer on the planet. However, through the process of following these steps, I have found that these things are the best I have to give the world. What if business leaders had this in mind as they seek to develop their employees? Want to solve the problem of having poor employee retention? Be an organization full of people who know that they are allowed to try new things, and progress through the steps that will eventually lead to them giving their very best to their companies.

Reigniting Passion in Your Personal Life:

Look in the mirror. Do you know what the best you looks like? Have you discovered the best you have to give? If I were to ask you, "What is your strength zone?" can you give me an honest answer? If you do answer me, are you certain that of all the things in the world there are to try, you know without a doubt you have discovered the thing that represents the best you have to give the world?

As you start on this journey to reignite passion in your life, much of this work is going to be done in your off hours. If you're a companion on this quest toward passion, your nights and weekends are going to be filled with new things, new adventures, and new experiences. When I was just starting out in the acting world I was on the set of *Lost* and *Hawaii Five-O* in my spare time. I took vacation time to engage in one of the things that was in my strength zone. Do you want this year to be better than last year? Use your spare time in efficient ways. I haven't owned a television since 2003. I had to reorganize my priorities and dedicate myself to the process of these eight steps. If you picked up this book because you're serious about reigniting the passion in your life, then there is going to have to be some give and take. Life is about balance and as with everything there a yin and a yang. If you're going to pursue your passion, then there are some other things that are going to have to wait. Leisure time changes. Priorities change. You change.

Reigniting Passion in Your Work Life:

People come up to me all the time and tell me that they or someone they know is completely lost in their career. They look to me because I literally wrote the book about finding and rediscovering their passion. It should be no surprise that the advice I give is to simply start out at Step 1 and try a bunch of stuff. It's amazing to me how simple these steps are but there are very few people who will actually engage in something as simple as trying new things. If you want to arrive at Step 3 and truly understand the best you have to give the world, you'll have to work with your employer and management to come up with a viable plan that leads you to it.

If you're a leader at your company or organization and want a workforce full of people who are giving their best to you, then it's time to open your mind to a new way of doing things around the office. Make it your goal to put your people in the right places, expose them to different roles within your company and become comfortable with changes that will lead to a more efficient workforce.

"We must believe that we are gifted for something, and that this thing, at whatever cost, must be attained."

–Marie Curie

Step 4: Ask Yourself If You're Passionate About It

When was the last time you got serious about your life and asked yourself about the things you are passionate about? Be real with me for a minute…. Have you ever paused and asked yourself if you're passionate about the things that you do?

Deloitte performed a recent study on employee passion and they found that 89 percent of American workers don't have passion for what they do.[1]

If the system of success that was handed to you by society is yielding only 11 percent passion, then I suggest you look elsewhere for cues on how to live your life. When you're passionate about what you're doing, it doesn't feel like work. When you're passionate about what you're doing, you'd do it all day long and you'd do it for free. When you're passionate, time

[1] Hagel, John, John Seely Brown, and Tamara Samoylova. *Unlocking the Passion of the Explorer: Report 1 of the 2013 Shift Index Series*. N.p.: Deloitte UP, 2013. Print.

flies and you have endless energy to do the things you're passionate about.

I'm 34 years old and I have found my passions in life. I first discovered that singing, keynote speaking and entertaining were in my strength zone when I was in junior high and high school. I discovered that they were my passions when I was 30 and on a world tour as an entertainer, emcee and vocalist. The lesson to learn here is that I was still asking myself what my passion was when I was 30 years old. By the time they reach age 30, most people have given up on finding their passion years ago.

I find that many people either:

> A) Never ask themselves what their passion is.
>
> B) Stop asking themselves that question way too early in life.

This is such a shame. In our society, it is as if we feel like we all need to "figure it out" so early in our lives. There is this undeniable pressure for teenagers to figure out what they're doing after high school. The pressure college students feel to pick a major and a career field they think they'll do well in is only increasing as the job market becomes more and more competitive.

However, around the ages of 22-24 we simply stop asking ourselves what we want in life. For most people, passion is not a conversation that gets more than a few moments of attention once every couple of years.

Why is this?

It's because life happens. Understandably, we all get caught up in the busy nature of our lives and before we know it we wake up and realize that we've spent the last 10 years of our lives working for a paycheck and we completely forgot about working towards our passion.

What we need to do is hit the "refresh" button in our lives from time to time, and ask ourselves if we're passionate about the things that we spend our time doing.

If the answer is no, then it's time to repeat Steps 1-3.

"Definiteness of purpose is the starting point of all achievement."

- W. Clement Stone

Step 5: Don't Stop Until You Find Your Passion

I'm 34 years old. By most estimations, I'm a young guy. During my school assemblies when I'm found in front of middle or high school students, I often talk about a concept called "The timeline of life." Picture this: I place cones on each side of the stage, one that represents birth and the other death. At 34 years of age, I find myself a little over a third of the way through my life expectancy. I place another set of cones in the teenage years, representing the period of life my audience is living in. Forgive the rough illustration, but it looks something like this:

Birth   Teenager   Me   Death

X   X X   X -----p-a-s-s-i-o-n-a-t-e--l-i-f-e----- X

I tell the students that from the time I was a teenager to today I have been fortunate enough to have some pretty amazing life experiences. I have acted with some of Hollywood's biggest stars in television shows like *Lost* and *Hawaii Five-O*. I have been in the same frame on the silver screen as giants of the industry like Liam Neeson. I have shared the stage with Director Peter Berg, performed for Rihanna, Brooks and Dunn and The Band Perry. I have been lucky enough to perform for staffers at the White

41

House and tour the world as an entertainer. Today, I sing for some of the largest crowds in America: 30,000 to 50,000 at a time. I ask the students where they think I learned to do all those things as an actor, entertainer and performer. Did I learn to do those things as a 34-year-old? Or did I first learn to do those things in my teenage years, when I was just discovering my likes and strengths in life? Of course, they all point to the teenage years. Then, I ask them where they are. When is the time when you are perfectly equipped to start discovering the likes, strengths and passions in your life? It is in the same chair they are sitting in now.

The great part about putting in the work necessary to find my passions early in life, is that now I have the wonderful opportunity to live the rest of my life as a passionate person from age 34 to the end of my life, whenever that may be.

But you may not be in high school, you may be much older. You may be thinking that it's too late for you. You may be thinking that you can't teach an old dog new tricks. I want to encourage you to start wherever you are today. It doesn't matter where you are on the timeline of life, you can begin the search for your passion and decide that you're not going to stop until you find it. Take it from a guy who lives his passions each and every day. It's worth it.

Don't wait until retirement to truly live. Don't wait until "someday" to get serious about your dreams, goals, visions and passions. That's not fair to yourself. It's not fair to your family and those who look up to you. Howard Thurman said it best:

"The ideal situation for a man or woman to die is to have family members standing with them as they cross over. But imagine, if you will, being on your death-bed, and standing around your bed are the ghosts of the ideas, the abilities, the talents, the gifts, the dreams given to you by life. That you, for whatever reason, never pursued those dreams. You never did anything with those ideas. You never used those talents. You never used those gifts. You never took advantage of those opportunities. And there they are, standing around your bed, looking at you before you take your last dying breath, looking at you with angry eyes saying, 'We came to you, and only you could have given us life and now we must die with you forever.'"

Kind of hits you right between the eyes, right? Or maybe it's like a punch in the gut. We all have to make a promise to ourselves that we won't stop until we find our passion. Have a little grit about you. Have a little determination. Make one of the most important decisions of your life and decide that the life that you live is going to be about passion. Tell yourself and everyone you know that you aren't going to settle for anything shy of loving what you do. Maybe you're going to have to rediscover your passion. Maybe you're reigniting your passion. Maybe you're finding it for the very first time. Wherever you are on the journey you have to know that passion for your life is out there somewhere. Just don't stop until you find it.

"Your work is going to fill a large part of your life, and the only way to be truly satisfied is to do what you believe is great work. And the only way to do great work is to love what you do. If you haven't found it yet, keep looking. Don't settle."   -Steve Jobs

Along the way there are going to be all kinds of distractions that are begging you to pause or abandon the journey. You're probably going to get married, then it's the kids, it's the keeping up with the Joneses. You'll pour yourselves into the lives of your children, which is fine by me, but I just want to caution you not to forget the balance of life, don't forget the yin and yang of your existence. Of the people who come up to me and are desperate for advice on how to find their passions in life, some of them undoubtedly had forgotten the balance required for a passion-filled life.

I spoke to a young father not long ago after one of my keynotes. He expressed to me his sense of urgency when it came to finding his passions in life. He was a young father of two and he said, "Mark, I have to live a passionate life... because one day I'm going to tell my kids to do the same and I'm setting the example for them." Brilliant. I can't think of a more meaningful reason to pursue one's passions than to think of the example you're setting for the young people in your life.

In my life I just couldn't settle for less than my absolute best. As a young teenager on the timeline of life I didn't know what my best looked like. Maybe it's a feeling. Maybe it's an intangible knowledge within that you have found the thing you are meant to do in this world. Maybe there are little signs and nudges. Maybe there are notifications from something greater than you that tell you that you have found it. I don't know if it's the same for all of us, but I do know that after over a dozen years of searching for my passions, I found them.

As I stated earlier, they call me the Forrest Gump of motivational speaking. Through this process of implementing Step 5 in my life, I have been to college, I have served in 13 states in AmeriCorps. I have tutored in inner city schools in Washington, D.C. and been shot at by gang members in what they used to call Murder City USA. I have fought wildland fires for the National Park Service in the Shenandoah Mountains and the Blue Ridge of Tennessee. We were called upon to be American Red Cross emergency responders at Ground Zero at the Pentagon in the days and weeks following 9/11/2001. I have built playgrounds in almost every major city in America and Habitat for Humanity houses in over a dozen states. I have consulted for the Department of Homeland Security, worked for the National Security Agency, been a Sergeant in the United States Air Force, toured the world as an entertainer, been an actor on *Lost* and *Hawaii Five-O*, and a stuntman, guest performer and credited actor in a $200 million dollar Universal Studios movie.

In my adult life I have had 15 jobs in the last 16 years. When I moved to North Fargo in 2013, that was the 21st place I had lived on planet earth since I graduated high school in 1999. Most people would look at those stats and tell me that this was the beginning of a failed life. Most people would question my checkered employment history and ask me when I was going to get serious about life and settle down. They would ask me when I would commit to something. What they didn't know is that I was simply progressing at my own pace through Steps 1-4. I was trying a bunch of stuff, finding out what I liked, and figuring out if I was any good at it. Then, every once in a while I would ask myself if this was my thing, if it was my love, my passion. If I answered no, then it was back to Step 1.

The journey to find my passion wasn't easy. For you, I hope it is much shorter with less heartache. But what if it isn't? What if your journey is longer and more difficult? So be it. It is still worth it. Don't settle. Please don't settle. Fight through the challenges. Fight through your friends and neighbors telling you that it's no use. Persevere through all the naysayers telling you that you are crazy. Because at the end of the rainbow you find yourself on your own timeline of life living the life of a passionate person, spending your time doing the things you love.

Whether it be at home or at work, the journey to find your passion is worth every penny and every passing day. Just don't stop the pursuit. Decide that your life is worth it. Don't stop until you find your passion.

"It is not the critic who counts; not the man who points out how the strong man stumbles, or where the doer of deeds could have done them better. The credit belongs to the man who is actually in the arena, whose face is marred by dust and sweat and blood; who strives valiantly; who errs, who comes short again and again, because there is no effort without error and shortcoming; but who does actually strive to do the deeds; who knows great enthusiasms, the great devotions; who spends himself in a worthy cause; who at the best knows in the end the triumph of high achievement, and who at the worst, if he fails, at least fails while daring greatly, so that his place shall never be with those cold and timid souls who neither know victory nor defeat."

-Teddy Roosevelt
"The Man in the Arena"
April 23, 1910

Step 6: Lean-in to Your Passion

As a motivational speaker, I always like to say that I'm not a "has been" who is out on the circuit talking about something that I did back in 1987. There's nothing wrong with the keynote speaker who celebrates and teaches from something extraordinary that happened long ago. However, as I travel the nation I believe that one of the things that my audiences appreciate most is that at the same time that I'm encouraging you to pursue your biggest goals and dreams – I'm out there swinging for the fences for my own as well. I'm not a has been, I'm an *am now* keynote speaker. I am a keynote speaker who not only talks the talk, but I walk the walk.

Last night (as I write this draft) I sang for 10,590 people. Two months from now I will perform with my 16-piece Sinatra style big band in front of a sold out house at the historic Fargo Theatre. I just cut my first studio album and should have the first CD in my hands in a month. Two days ago I communicated with the Minnesota Twins about singing the National Anthem for their playoff games (although, unfortunately the Twins ended up missing the playoffs). A month ago I was invited to audition for the Cleveland Cavaliers to sing for their crowd at Quicken Loans Arena for the 2015-2016 NBA season. One of the best WNBA teams in the league, The Minnesota Lynx, recently allowed me to be a guest performer for them at the Target Center in Minneapolis, and they have informed me that I'll be able to do the same for the bright young team we call the Minnesota Timberwolves. A few weeks ago I was in touch with the NCAA and my name is being tossed around at the office that coordinates all the in-venue presentations for the NCAA Championships for various sports around the nation. It was just a year ago that I sang for the Minnesota Vikings at their home opener in front of over 52,000 fans live and over 17 million people around the world, live on CBS Sports. I just signed our second contract to be the full-time National Anthem singer for the University of North Dakota Men's Hockey program for every home game at the Ralph Engelstad Arena in Grand Forks, North Dakota. To my knowledge, I'm one of the only, if not the only, full-time National Anthem singer for any NCAA Men's hockey program anywhere in the nation.

As a keynote speaker, in 2014 I delivered 82 keynotes and had 56 singing appearances on my calendar and performed live for over a half million people around the nation. In 2015 I will deliver over 125 keynotes and just finished a couple of keynote gigs with Microsoft. I speak for billion dollar companies, state, regional and nationwide conferences, and even the local Boy Scouts or small nonprofit fundraisers. This month, I traveled 7,200 miles behind the wheel of my car and had 25 speaking gigs in three states.

Why do I do all of this? Because I have done the work necessary to find my passion; now that I have found it, I lean-in and do it all the time. I never get sick of it, because it is what I love. If you're lucky enough to be a part of the minority who loves what they do and are passionate about their work, then do it all the time.

Employers, managers, CEOs… which person do you want working for you? The person who is passionate about their work and the things they do for you and your company? Or do you want the burned out, frustrated, bored person on your payroll? Allow your people to progress through Steps 1-5 and then Step 6 is the payoff. It's the time where all your hard work and flexibility really starts to show dividends. Of course, I think that you'll recognize a difference and a "return on your investment" long before Step 6. I think your people will express a higher level of satisfaction at work once they realize that you're allowing them the flexibility to progress through Steps 1-5 at their own pace.

Just imagine an entire workforce who is now leaning-in to their passions. They have discovered their strengths and they are doing those things for your company. People are excited about what they do and your organization is reaching new heights because for the first time in your history, there is a core group of employees who have taken the steps necessary to grow, learn about themselves, and stretch beyond their comfort zone in order to arrive at the destination of passion.

Just imagine what would be possible if you implemented these steps in your employee culture.

Listen to the words of my buddy Hank. He captures it pretty well when he says:

"If one advances confidently in the direction of his dreams, and endeavors to live the life which he has imagined, he will meet with success unexpected in common hours." -Henry David Thoreau

Advance confidently. Lean-in. Hit the gas. If you have followed these steps and are fortunate enough to be a part of the population who is passionate about what they do, then do it all the time. Give the world your best. You'll meet success.

Step 7: Take the Money and Run

If you are fortunate enough to get paid to do the things you are passionate about, then you win. Don't feel guilty about it, take the money and run. You have found Willy Wonka's golden ticket.

Managers, leaders, CEOs, this note is for you. You're already paying your people, now the missing part of the equation is to make sure that everyone in your employ is passionate about what they do for you and your company. How do you do this? Create a company culture that revolves around Steps 1-4. Don't have a workforce full of passionate people? Allow them to try new things. Soon they'll find out what they like, then start identifying the things that fall in their strength zone. I'm sure you won't have to start over at Step 1 with everyone – after all, if they were talented enough to get hired at your organization, I'm sure that they have some idea of what their best is. But it just might take a little bit of cooperation and collaboration on your part to get them to the point where they truly feel as if they're giving their best to you and are getting paid to do what they love.

Reigniting Passion in Your Personal Life:

When someone comes up to me and asks what they need to do in order to live a life filled with passion, the first thing that I talk about is their finances. This is the step called "Take the Money and Run," right? Money is most often the thing that will keep people from pursing their passion.

The bottom line is this; you might be getting paid six figures for the job you have today. If you're like most people and find that your passion lies in another realm, you don't have the freedom to change career fields and pursue a career that might pay less, because you have consistently increased your lifestyle to match your current income. Let's be honest, when most of us get a raise we find some way to spend that extra money. If you're a six-figure income earner now and you decide that being a coffee shop barista is your new found passion… you probably can't pursue that, because you have bills to pay.

From the beginning of our adult lives we are overextended and we can't help ourselves from doing our best to keep up with the Joneses. Credit cards, mortgages we can't afford, car payments, student loan debt, monthly payments etc. Of course, I'm not suggesting that we all have to live in poverty, but I am saying that almost every person I speak to is overextended to the point that their finances would be the first thing that prevents them from pursing their passion.

Allow me to illustrate. Let's say that you have progressed through the steps and now you've discovered or reignited one of your passions. Listen to me now, ***you might not be good enough at the thing you're passionate about to get paid for it.*** You might have to spend years at the back of the line or the bottom rung until you become proficient enough at your passion in order to get people to pay you for it. Simple example: If you are currently in accounting, but you find that your true passion lies in the arena of human resources... you might not possess the credentials or skills necessary to be paid at the same level in your company. It might take some night schooling or some consulting work part-time on your nights and weekends in order to build a resume impressive enough to get paid for your new found passion.

You've got to be patient with this step. Many people think that now that they've discovered their true passions in life that the correct move is to quit their job and go full-time with this new endeavor. I am a believer in this mantra: Just because you're passionate about what you do doesn't mean that you should abandon good planning. Pump the brakes for a second. My journey to live a passion-filled life took me over a dozen years. It took patience. It took time. It took me years and years of singing, performing, and speaking to rooms of ten and twenty and the occasional audience of over a hundred to get good enough for stadiums full of people to ask me to grab the mic.

Take my National Anthem rendition for example. I started singing that song for the Ortonville High School football team for the players, coaches and about 100 people on the sidelines. I performed my rendition of the Star Spangled Banner at military retirements and promotions for audiences of 30-40 for years before Universal Studios asked me to sing for them. I was 33 years old before my first stadium full of people called; in fact, it was June 20th, 2014 before I broke 20,000 in an audience.

Sometimes you'll have to spend years and years in the proverbial audition rooms of your life in order to become good enough to get paid for the thing you do. You might have to spend even more time cutting your teeth at the back of the line until you can get paid well enough to do the thing you love full-time. Those are the rare few who can excel in the realm of their passion at the level that they can make a full-time living doing that thing.

The process of transitioning to full-time income that is derived from your passion sometimes takes time. It takes patience. It takes dedication.

I spent 15 years of my adult life giving the occasional best man speech or fill-in sermon for the local pastor at the church. There were times when I would grab the mic at a wedding when I wasn't even the best man. I would tell some funny stories about the couple and during these impromptu speeches I started learning what worked with audiences and what didn't. I had probably delivered keynote speeches for 50,000 people before a company like Microsoft asked me to speak to their people.

Be excited that you have found a passion in your life. Be equally as patient with yourself as you work through the process of becoming good enough to be able to take the money and run.

Reigniting Passion in Your Work Life:

Employers, don't worry about guiding your people toward the destination of finding their passion with the thought that they might leave you once they do. I guarantee if you were the person or organization that led them to find their life's passion – even if they do end up leaving your company someday down the road - they will always look up on you with favor because you are the reason they are where they are. I once heard John Maxwell talk about a discussion he had with a point guard on an NBA team. They were talking about the importance of celebrating the small victories with your teammates. The example he used was the moment when the point guard makes a flawless pass that leads to a score. John Maxwell said that you should always look in the direction of the player who scored, and acknowledge their hand in the small victory. The point guard then said, "What if they're not looking?" John said, ***"They'll always be looking."***

The same holds true with you and your people. If you give them the opportunity of a lifetime to discover the thing that ends up being their passion, they will never forget you. They, just like the person who scored in the big game, will always be looking your way. Life happens. People move on. We don't live in a world where a person works 40 years with one company and then gets a gold watch at retirement. Today's workforce is hungry. They're in search of more. Millennials in the workforce are leading the charge and they demand that they love what they do. My best advice is to create an employee culture that allows the freedom for your people to progress through Steps 1-4 until they find the things that they're passionate about.

If your people do leave you as a part of this process, then so be it. I believe that if your people feel so strongly that they need to be in a different place, then it is your job as the leader to understand where they are and encourage them along their way. If they need to move on, let them move on. You don't want to be the reason they're being held back anyway. Invest your time in the personnel you can nurture and grow long term with the goal of having an entire team of people who have arrived at Destination Passion under your roof.

If you can get paid to do the things you love, then you win. If you're gainfully employed today but don't feel that passion... then progress through the steps until you have found a way to reignite that passion. Your future self will thank you.

Step 8: Everything Is Possible

If you have arrived at the place in your life where you can stand up and say that you are a passionate person who is pursuing and involved in the things you're passionate about, then why would you believe that only a few things are possible? Why not believe that the best is possible, that everything is possible? What have you got to lose?

Many people read my fancy bio that chronicles the highlights of a career performing in 22 countries and 44 states for over a million people. They read about being on some of the hottest shows on television and in blockbuster movies. The story continues with performances for the Supreme Allied Commander of NATO Europe, for staffers at the White House, and American legends like the Tuskegee Airmen. I've been featured in almost every major newspaper in America, including the *Miami Herald*, the *Washington Times*, the *Houston Chronicle* and the *Dallas-Fort Worth Star-Telegram*. People say, "How is it that over the course of your life you have consistently been able to come up with all these neat opportunities year after year?"

I tell them that there is really only one explanation for the things that have come my way these past 15+ years.

Have you ever gone car shopping and you find yourself this beautiful new model that you've never seen before? You go home and tell your spouse about this rare color, cherry red... let's call it a red Jeep Cherokee. So you decide that you're going to go buy this red Jeep Cherokee and you're going to be the only one on the block with this new beauty. You drive it off the lot. What do you see for the next three weeks as you drive around town?? Red Jeep Cherokees!! They're everywhere! They're at the stoplight next to you! They're parked next to you at the store! Bob in accounting has the exact same one!

Here's my question: Were those red Jeep Cherokees there before? Of course they were! They were always there. You just weren't focused on them.

The best way I can explain the past 15 years of my career is to say this. I see opportunities in the realm of my strength zone and my passions – just like you see red Jeep Cherokees. I see these opportunities everywhere. There is no lack of opportunity here in America. We live in the land of opportunity. Maybe the difference between me and the next guy is that I believe that the opportunity is there for me. I believe that it is possible, for me. Someone is going to get that part in the show, it might as well be me. Someone is going to sing that song, it might as well be me.

Someone is going to be on the marquee on Saturday night, it might as well be me. Someone is going to deliver that keynote at Microsoft, it might as well be me.

I believe everything is possible and you should too. This is the level of thinking that we have to embrace if we want to achieve the things that we dream of and live the life we have imagined. You have to embrace this way of thinking. Now that I've found my passions in the realm of speaking, performing, entertaining and writing… I have expanded my idea of what is possible. Everything.

I believe that this book could be a best-seller. If it's not this book, I still believe I have a best-selling book in me.

I believe that as a motivational speaker, I will be the next Tony Robbins. I'm 34 years old and I have plenty of time to sharpen my skills and improve my ideas.

I believe that as a Sinatra-style singer I will perform with my big band or orchestra on the Vegas strip. I believe I will win Grammys and become a platinum selling recording artist.

I believe I will sing the National Anthem at the Super Bowl. Someone is going to sing that song at the big game… it might as well be me.

Imagine if your people thought at this level. Imagine if your people began to believe that everything was possible. I believe that people succeed or fail based on the way they think. All people really need is someone to show them that it is possible. If you don't have anyone in your life who is showing you what is possible, please allow me to be that person. I'm going to do the things I just listed above. I don't think it's arrogant, I don't think it's cocky. I just know that one human being could do those things. It might as well be me.

I believe your people deserve to think at this level. I believe that you deserve to change and enhance your thinking to the level of everything is possible. Life at the level of everything is possible is fun. It's exciting. This is the realm where dreams come true on a regular basis. This is the realm where you dominate the competition and you win. You win big.

But what if you don't currently believe that everything is possible? No problem. I get it. At one point in my life I didn't believe *anything* was possible. What I needed in order to get myself to this level of thinking was a series of small victories over time. Win. It doesn't matter how long it takes you to win; eventually, I believe if you stick with it long enough, you'll win. Then your next goal is to win again. In between wins, you'll lose a time or two, but learn from those losses, learn about what you did in order to win, and then win again. We all need this series of small victories. Eventually, you'll be able to pick something that seems impossible – but you'll win. Now you're on the road to believing that everything is possible. Then, for the rest of your life nobody will be able to convince you of anything else, you'll just believe everything is possible and you'll just keep winning.

If you can get yourself to the level of everything is possible thinking, you are now a dangerous element. If you can empower your people to this level, you're piloting the unstoppable force. I think we've all heard enough of the naysayers and the people who think that life is about limits and we all need to be aware of what we can't do and what we can't have.

What if you and I got together and decided that everything is possible? Just imagine the things we could accomplish. Just imagine the wins we could rack up. Everything *is* possible. I believe it. You can too.

"To give your PASSIONATE self to the world is the greatest gift you can give the world."

-Mark J. Lindquist

Afterword

My journey to discover my passions in life took me over 15 years. I don't know where you are on the epic odyssey to find or reignite your passions. Maybe you're a few months away or maybe it will take you as long as it took me. Most likely, the journey won't be without a few bumps in the road. Most likely, it will seem like a lost cause at times. I often found myself facing a mountain of doubt, wondering if I was ever going to find it. However, I just want to take this time to encourage you and let you know that there is indeed a pot of gold at the end of the rainbow.

Do you know that old saying, "If you do what you love, you'll never work a day in your life?" It sounds a bit corny, and an old timer or two has probably given you this sage advice once or twice throughout your lifetime. But I really think there is wisdom in this phrase. I feel so fortunate that I can speak from experience and tell you that once you find the things that you love, the things that you are passionate about, then it never feels like work.

I hope you can find a way to implement these 8 simple steps into your life. I hope that this book is your first step on the journey to reignite the passion in your life.

As Dr. Martin Luther King Jr. said, "You don't have to see the whole staircase. Just take the first step."

It's called, "Passion! 8 Steps to Reignite Yours."

Just take the first step.

Step 1: Try a Bunch of Stuff

Step 2: Find Out What You Like

Step 3: Find Your Strength Zone

Step 4: Ask Yourself If You're Passionate About It

Step 5: Don't Stop Until You Find Your Passion

Step 6: Lean-in to Your Passion

Step 7: Take the Money and Run

Step 8: Everything is Possible

69

Making Our Impact on the World

I give my passionate self to the world as often as I possibly can. As a motivational speaker, entertainer, and entrepreneur, I seek to make my impact on the world in many ways. Primarily, I deliver keynote speeches at conferences and conventions, for corporate meetings and employee gatherings. I also deliver school assemblies at middle and high schools and I speak at youth conferences, colleges and Young Professionals Networks. Another one of my passions is found in the realm of volunteerism; for that reason, I also speak for non-profit groups, civic organizations and service clubs.

My business manager, long-time best friend, and like-minded champion of passion, Mr. Jared L. Bye is the one who makes all of this happen. He is truly the "brains behind our operation" and makes it possible for our companies to make the impact that we do. We speak to people as young as 5th graders all the way up to the CEOs and business leaders at billion dollar companies.

When we are out on the road and on stage, you'll find us delivering keynotes on three different topics:

Passion. Service. Gratitude.

At Breath Is Limited Motivational Speaking and Entertainment, LLC we are in the business of "Advancing Ideas... Igniting Passion." Our goal is to lead as many people as possible toward the discovery of their passions. We seek to inspire, entertain, and lead others toward their passionate self.

Here is our full topic list as of Winter of 2015:
Also found at www.BreathIsLimited.com

Passion! 8 Steps to Reignite Yours
Based on our book "Passion! 8 Steps to Reignite Yours," Mark will deliver a message that is the perfect opening or closing keynote for your event or conference. Mark will either start your conference off on the right foot or send your people out the door on fire. The #1 issue that Mark is asked to address is a workforce that needs a jolt in the arm. He finds that employees need to re-ignite the passion that brought them into the workforce in the first place. Audience members will have the opportunity to hear Mark teach straight from the playbook he has developed in 26 countries and all 50 states. Suitable for Corporate Audiences, Conference Keynotes, Sales Meetings, Managers Meetings, Young Professionals Networks, and College Audiences.

Service, My Way of Life

This keynote is perfect for the organization that is experiencing employee burnout, volunteer fatigue or the company that has a stressed out workforce. Mark finds that people come to conferences looking for some type of renewed inspiration that they can take back to their place of work and re-engage with their life's work with renewed fervor. Mark's stories of service all over the globe help prepare your people to make a deeper commitment to their mission at work and in life. He touches on principles such as, "A life well lived is a life spent giving back to those who have given so much to you" and "If a true sense of value is to be yours, then it must come through service." Suitable for Corporate Audiences, Conference Keynotes, Civic Organizations, Youth Groups, School Assemblies and Corporate Community Involvement departments.

Gratitude. Live it.

During this riveting keynote address, Mark will inject a profound sense of gratitude into your organizational culture and leave your people with a common language to build upon. Mark will provide a toolkit of ideas that will help people carry their gratitude with them into the future. Following this talk, audience members have called loved ones they haven't called for years; individuals who weren't on speaking terms found a way to mend fences and move forward. Mark will have your people diving down into the deepest roots of themselves - and at the end of the day your people will be undeniably changed. Suitable for Corporate Audiences, Conference Keynotes, School Assemblies and Classroom Presentations.

CFO asks CEO: "What happens if we invest in developing our people and then they leave us?"

CEO: "What happens if we don't and they stay?"

Breath Is Limited Motivational Speaking and Entertainment Conference Services

The compliment we most often receive is, "Mark was the best hour of our conference!"

We offer:

- Keynotes
- Breakout Sessions
- Half-Day Trainings
- World-Class Emceeing
- Live Sinatra-Style Entertainment (Solo, 45 Minute Set)
- Live Sinatra-Style Entertainment (Live 16 Piece Band, 60-90 Minute Set)

Few speakers or entertainers can make an impact at your upcoming conference in the many ways Mark J. Lindquist can.

Find us at www.BreathIsLimited.com!!

About the Author Mark J. Lindquist

Mark J. Lindquist is a nationally recognized motivational speaker, world-touring entertainer, lead singer of the Mark J. Lindquist Big Band, as well as the author of the books, "Passion! 8 Steps to Find Yours" and "Service! My Way of Life." Mark has performed live for over 1,000,000 people in 22 countries and 44 states throughout his career. As an actor, he has appeared in ABC's *LOST*, CBS' *Hawaii Five-O* and the Universal Studios movie *Battleship*.

He has performed for Grammy winning artists, Academy Award nominated actors, foreign dignitaries around the world as well as staffers at the White House. Mark has been featured on CNN.com, C-Span, *The Washington Post*, *The Washington Times*, *The Dallas-Fort Worth Star Telegram*, *The San Francisco Chronicle*, *The Miami Herald*, *The Houston Chronicle* and the *Korea Today Newspaper* (Seoul, South Korea).

Mark has shared the stage with former U.S. Attorney General Janet Reno, Senator John McCain, Magic Johnson, Edward James Olmos, Grammy-Award winning artists Rihanna, Brooks and Dunn and Brandy, The Band Perry, Dierks Bentley, Academy-

Award nominated actor Liam Neeson, CEO Bob Nardelli (Home Depot), Steve Case (AOL/Time Warner), Ken Thompson (Wachovia), Jeff Swartz (Timberland) and Ben and Jerry (Ben and Jerry's Ice Cream).

Throughout his entertainment career, Mark has performed for the Tuskegee Airmen, the Secretary of the Interior Gayle Norton, Secretary of Commerce Don Evans, Secretary of Labor Elaine Chao, Members of Congress, Sargent Shriver, Mia Hamm, Tony Stewart, The Washington Redskins, The Atlanta Falcons, and The New York Giants (NFL), the Florida Panthers (NHL), the Washington Nationals (MLB), the NCAA, Universal Studios and The Supreme Allied Commander of NATO Europe.

Currently, Mark travels the country delivering keynote addresses for businesses, colleges, young professionals' networks, conferences and school assemblies. He also performs the National Anthem for collegiate and professional sports teams and is the full-time National Anthem singer for the University of North Dakota Men's Hockey program as well as a guest performer for the College World Series, WE Fest, The Minnesota Twins, The Minnesota Lynx, The Los Angeles Dodgers and The Minnesota Vikings.

Mark co-founded Breath Is Limited Motivational Speaking and Entertainment, LLC in order to advance ideas and ignite passion all over the world.

Mark is a former AmeriCorps member, a former Sergeant in the United States Air Force and an Afghanistan War Veteran who currently lives in Fargo, North Dakota.

Mark J. Lindquist

Jared L. Bye

80

About the Co-Author Jared L. Bye

Jared L. Bye is a serial entrepreneur who currently owns, controls and manages Breath is Limited Motivational Speaking and Entertainment and JLB Talent Management. In his role at Breath is Limited Motivational Speaking and Entertainment, Jared represents clients throughout the United States. He consults with speakers and entertainers, negotiates contracts on the client's behalf, and books gigs for the speaker/entertainer after a brief probationary period. Jared works with speakers who are brand new to the business as well as seasoned veterans of the stage. No matter the level of experience, Jared's managerial expertise has proven to be an invaluable component of a performer's success.

As Mark J. Lindquist's business manager, Jared is the co-author of this book, he is a marketing consultant, and lead speechwriter who co-wrote two TED Talks since 2013. Together, they have impacted over 17.5 million people around the globe with their work.

Jared currently lives in Fargo, North Dakota with his wife Aftin and their two children.

About the Co-Author Patrick O'Shaughnessy

Patrick O'Shaughnessy is a Little Rock, Arkansas based world-touring entertainer and motivational speaker who has performed live for over 250,000 troops and their families at 124 United States Military installations around the globe. Patrick has served as a consultant for one of the longest running entertainment troupes in America, Tops in Blue.

He has been a guest performer for the American Chamber of Commerce in Abu Dhabi, United Arab Emirates; the Washington Nationals major league baseball team; and staffers at the White House on President Barack Obama's 50th birthday. He is also a singer and production manager for the Mark J. Lindquist Big Band.

Patrick co-wrote the TED Talk "The Most Uninformed Decision You Will Ever Make" and is currently in the process of producing his first studio album.

Staff Sergeant O'Shaughnessy is an Afghanistan war veteran and current reservist in the United States Air Force Reserve, based out of Little Rock Air Force Base.

Patrick O'Shaughnessy

Contacting Mark, Jared and Breath Is Limited Motivational Speaking and Entertainment:

You can contact the business office at Breath Is Limited Motivational Speaking and Entertainment, LLC at:

3120-Z 25th Street South
Suite 160
Fargo, ND 58103

You may email us at:
Mark@BreathIsLimited.com

Jared@BreathIsLimited.com

Websites: www.BreathIsLimited.com
                www.MarkJLindquist.com

Twitter: @MarkJLindquist

Facebook: Mark J. Lindquist

Instagram: MarkJLindquist

Mark's List of 10:

1. Singing

2. Speaking

3. Meeting people

4. Traveling

5. Working on my latest project or dream

6. Skiing

7. Hiking

8. Talking to mom

9. Setting and achieving goals

10. Making someone's day

Passion! Reignite Yours.

66082558R00052